ROCK THE BOAT

Boats, Cabins and Homes on the Water

gestalten

WHY LIVE AFLOAT?

Saunalautta, pages 156–158

Bert's Barge, pages 5–9

Waking up to the glint of sunlight on the water; taking a spontaneous after-dinner dip; swapping your morning commute for a riverside stroll. These are pleasures that transcend the boundaries of age, taste and budget—which is why there are enough different ways of living on water to suit anyone, anywhere.

Once relegated to the fringes of society—the domain of either the very poor or the super-rich—houseboats are experiencing a resurgence in popularity as people recognise the multitude of freedoms offered by a life on the water. In a world where the ability to disengage from the constant whirr of modern life is a rare luxury, a houseboat provides its owner with a chance to reconnect with nature and

reclaim a sense of independence that is becoming increasingly difficult to achieve on land. Along with the aesthetic advantages of open space, light and a lack of background traffic rumble, a life afloat also offers the freedom to release your moorings and leave behind familiar terra firma whenever the mood takes you. Who knows what discoveries might arise from this chance for spontaneous adventure?

Living in a floating home offers the opportunity for new modes of self-expression that range from DIY minimalism to non-conformist luxury. This artistic vision is often integrated with environmental awareness: many architects, engineers, and urban planners are exploring ways to

Whim Houseboat, pages 176–179

2

Gloria, pages 228–233

combat climate change, urban densification, and overuse of resources. The Swale community garden in New York City, for example, invites visitors to grow and pick their own food from the trees on board, while the owners of Freedom Cove, an off-grid floating island in British Columbia, Canada, use recycled materials and sustainable energy to power their lifestyle. As a possible answer to rising sea levels and flooding, floating homes can adjust as water levels change, working with the water instead of against it as grounded buildings do.

The myriad possibilities of living on water today range in size and scope, from cozy narrowboats cruising England's canals, to the massive "Maritol", a Nordic car ferry reimagined as a startup incubator in San Francisco Bay. Houseboats also differ in mobility and autonomy, from permanent moorings in urban houseboat communities to design-forward dwellings providing modern nomads off-grid comfort for weeks on end, as seen in Portugal on the „FloatWing" Houseboat, which can be energy self-sufficient for up to six months. Several of the featured houseboats were once cargo-carrying vessels that still bear traces of their nautical history.

Testing the waters of living afloat has never been easier, with plenty of temporary options open to those looking to dip a toe in. Liveaboard leisure can be as simple as hooking up your car to the "Sealander", an amphibious trailer that morphs into a boat, or unplugging for a few nights at floating vacation village "Village Flottant" in France, which is known for extraordinary bird-watching experiences. Casting the net further, you might venture off to an underwater hotel suite along the Tanzanian coast, or embark on a seafaring spa tour of the Arctic Circle.

Are you tempted by a life afloat?

Retrouvius Floating Cabin, pages 254–263

It's time to take a chance, get your feet wet, and do something a little bit different. But first things first—dive into Rock the Boat, and explore the many inspiring ways to enjoy life on the water.

ALL ABOARD! ∼

BOUTIQUE BARGE

Those in search of a unique stay in London should head to Bert's Barges—a floating boutique hotel suite in narrowboat form. Moored on Regent's Canal in East London's hip borough of Hackney, the boat measures 14.63 × 3.35 m (48 × 11 ft.). Designed with a sense of

Scandinavian chic, its monochrome interior is beautified with vintage mid-century furniture and luxury amenities: a full kitchen, walk-in shower, under-floor heating, wood-burning stove, and king-sized bed with down and linen bedding. The floating B&B is a spin-off project for interiors company Bert&May. The idea came about when founder Lee Thornley needed a part-time base in London. The location of the company's showroom on the canal inspired the idea of having a houseboat there: "I looked out at the water and thought, 'why not build something beautiful to go on it?'" A steel-framed custom-built barge was outfitted with reclaimed clapboard walls, handmade encaustic tiles, and engineered flooring, all from the Bert&May catalog. The vessel in Hackney is the first of a planned fleet of four boutique hotel barges to be established in London, York, and Bristol. ～

"I LOOKED OUT AT THE WATER AND THOUGHT, 'WHY NOT BUILD SOMETHING BEAUTIFUL TO GO ON IT?'"

FISHING VESSEL TO ARCTIC SPA

Visitors can take in the Northern Lights from an on-deck saltwater hot tub, dive into crystal clear Arctic waters from a 7 m-high (23 ft.) diving tower, or simply relax aboard the "Vulkana," a sea-faring spa based in the northern Norwegian city of Tromsø. The former fishing boat,

built in 1957, underwent a lavish transformation led by Finnish architect Sami Rintala of Rintala Eggertsson Architects and Norwegian boat builder Gunnar Eldjarn. The "Vulkana" is outfitted with a Finnish sauna boasting panoramic views, a Turkish steam bath, and a wood-clad lounge with a fireplace and skylight. Visitors can drop in by the hour to use the spa facilities, or book various cruises along Norway's coastline, taking in the wonders of the Arctic Circle. The 22 m (72 ft.) boat has seven cabins sleeping up to 12 people, and an on-board chef to prepare locally sourced Nordic meals. According to co-owner Erlend Larsson, the idea of "Vulkana" came to him while relaxing with a friend on a small boat. "We thought how much more relaxing it »»

» would be if we built a sauna inside it. Then we thought, if we have a sauna we might as well have a hot tub, and if we have a hot tub, we have to have a hammam. One thing led to another..." ~

AIRBNB'S FLAGSHIP DWELLING

Making a show of the unique experiences to be had through home sharing, Airbnb launched a branded houseboat on the Thames River in London. The campaign in May 2015 aimed to raise awareness of revised laws permitting Londoners to share their homes for up to 90 days annually. Designed by Nick and Steve Tidball with TBWA London, the 70-ton, 8-m-high (26 ft.) two-bedroom house included a working bathroom

and a garden with real grass and an apple tree. Water pipes and electricity generators were hidden in the roof and beneath the dog house, and the garden walls reinforced with steel to withstand waves. Despite looking like a two-to three-level building from the outside, the house consisted of a single level with a raised floor to disguise its floating base. After being pulled by a tugboat along the Thames for a week, the house was docked at Putney Pier, where people could win a stay at the house with a multi-course dinner, wellness treatment, and a sunrise breakfast. ～

A RAFT FOR EVERYBODY

Soomaa is a national park in Estonia that is subject to seasonal flooding, usually in spring. For weeks, the water covers fields, forests, and roads,

disrupting connections with the rest of the world. Locals and visitors use boats to navigate the altered territory, but a group of students went further to address the needs of the people in the area. As part of a 10-day summer program with the Estonian Academy of Arts Interior Architecture department, they investigated new types of floating space they could build in response to the area's changing and challenging environment. Tutored by Finnish architect and artist Sami Rintala, Serbian architect Pavle Stamenovic, and Estonian architecture office b210, the young participants used spruce timber and metal barrels to build a »»

» floating structure accommodating a shelter, a fireplace, and a sauna. Instead of relying on laptops, the young participants were encouraged to sketch their ideas on scraps of paper or wood. Although the sauna did not withstand the test of time, the main structure and adjacent fire-place, together dubbed "Veetee" (Estonian for waterway), are now open to the public as part of the local forest infrastructure. ∿

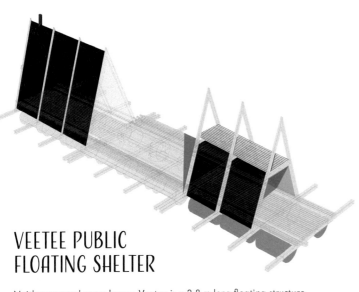

VEETEE PUBLIC FLOATING SHELTER

Neither a vessel nor a house, Veetee is a 3.8-m-long floating structure that enables its passengers to embark on an atmospheric journey through their surroundings. **Above:** sketch of the original prototype includes an additional floating sauna.

CONTEMPLATING NATURE ON WALDEN RAFT

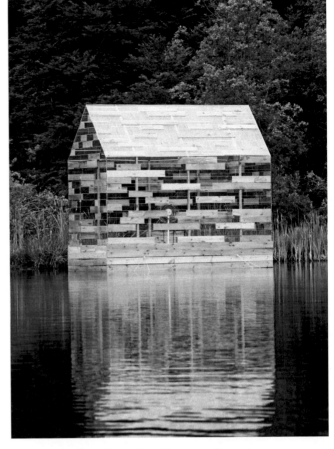

Inspired by the cabin Henry David Thoreau built in the woods of Walden Pond in 1845, Elise Morin and Florent Albinet created "Walden Raft," a floating, navigable cabin. Taking roughly the same dimensions as Thoreau's cabin, the raft, measuring 4 × 2.5 × 4 m (13 × 8 × 13 ft.), was presented as a public installation on Lac de Gayme in central France—situated at the same latitude as the site of Thoreau's cabin across the Atlantic. Crafted from reclaimed wood and recyclable acrylic glass and mounted on polyethylene floats, the combination of materials "brings transparency to the construction while maintaining its protective function," according to the designers. The materials combined to express the interaction between interior and exterior, pointing to the relationship between society and nature. Visitors could move the raft along a cable strung from the shore to an anchor in the middle of the lake by rotating a central reel. For the designers, "'Walden Raft' is a non-space whose position is unceasingly readjusted. Neither public property, nor private, nor entirely outside the world, nor entirely interiorized, it is an intermediate space, a lookout post where one can see while accepting to be seen." ~

FLOATING CABIN – *Volga River, Kalyazin, Russia*
Designed by DublDom

FROM RUSSIA WITH LOVE

Founded by architect Ivan Ovchinnikov, Russian company DublDom produces modular timber-framed homes designed to be quickly and easily installed on land as well as water. Available in a

variety of standard sizes and configurations, each house is delivered by truck and is fully insulated, wired, and plumbed, with all fixtures installed. Engineering systems are designed to be connected to outlets on the ground but can function independently with an electric generator. With production facilities in Kazan and the Czech Republic, DublDom has plans to expand to the United States. Customers can specify the colors of the walls and ceilings and also add features, such as special roof cladding, extra insulation, and furniture—the architects offer their own »

» line of wood furniture to match the style of their homes. The DublDom houseboat pictured here consists of three modules: two house modules and the veranda module, with a total living area of 26 m² (280 ft.²). Moored on the Volga River north of Moscow, it was installed in a single day upon metal pontoons provided by the client, and serves as a guest house at Hotel Paluba. ~

FROM FERRY
TO FLOATING SPA

FLOATING SPA – *St. Lawrence River, Montreal, Canada*
Designed by Sid Lee Architecture

Wellness and water go hand in hand—the term "spa" derives from the Belgian town of Spa where a natural spring with curative properties was discovered during the Middle Ages. Some consider the word to be an acronym for the Latin phrase *sanitas per aquam* meaning "health through water." This background is what Geneviève Emond had in mind when looking for a location to expand her family's spa business to Montreal. "We wanted an exterior space by the water, a place with its own vibe. Finding that place in Montreal was a challenge, and that's how the idea of doing it on a boat came about," she explains. When she and her family heard about a retired ferry for sale, they jumped at the occasion to buy it, even before knowing where exactly it could be anchored.

Built in 1951, the 52 m (170 ft.) vessel began its life on the water, carrying passengers between Sorel and Berthier, Quebec, well into the »

"WE WANTED AN EXTERIOR SPACE BY THE WATER, A PLACE WITH ITS OWN VIBE."

» next decade. In 1967 it became a traveling arts center, hosting shows on the Richelieu River for decades. It included a theater, restaurant, bars, and cabins for staff and performers. The last show was performed in 2007, and the Emond family acquired the worn vessel a year later, entrusting the ambitious project of its transformation into an experiential floating spa to Jean Pelland of Sid Lee Architecture, with whom they have collaborated on other spas in Quebec. According to Pelland, "it was an ugly duckling that could have ended up as scrap metal somewhere, but we made it a tribute to adapting architecture."

The conversion was a multidisciplinary undertaking that lasted 30 months, involving architects, interior and graphic designers, naval »

» engineers, plumbers, carpenters, electricians, upholsterers, and many more. The biggest constraint on the project was what made it so special: "its very nature, that of a floating steel structure," explain the architects. "Everything had to be precisely designed and calculated: the location of each space, the selection of materials, and the integration of services." The hull underwent extensive repair and modification to expand its carrying capacity and buoyancy. In addition to avoiding the high costs of maintaining a moving boat, removing the engine freed up space for the technical and mechanical infrastructure, and most importantly, the changing rooms. The large main bridge was able to accommodate an additional floor, where treatment rooms, a reception area, café, and two relaxation

lounges are located. The upper bridge was completely overhauled to make room for baths, saunas, a hammam, relaxation spaces, and outdoor decking. Components were fabricated to precise specification so as not to waste space, and adjustments made to decrease weight. Instead of the wood lockers that were initially desired, lighter, narrow-gauge steel was used. Invoking the feel of an ocean liner, more than 650 portholes of »

» various sizes were installed, offering natural light, scenic views, and architectural texture. The ship has its own water treatment facility and an innovative open geothermal loop that the relatively constant temperature of the water in the Saint Lawrence River aids in heating and cooling. On the outside, the boat reflects its industrial setting, with black-painted steel panels, which are warmed by cedar wood accents. Inside, relaxation and treatment spaces are almost entirely black or very dark gray, inviting

BLACK-PAINTED STEEL PANELS ARE WARMED BY CEDAR WOOD ACCENTS.

visitors on a quiet, contemplative journey. As guests travel closer to the top deck, the spaces open up with more light and with a greater connection to nature and the surrounding waters.

For the name of the spa, "Bota Bota, spa-sur-l'eau," "the primary concept was to create a name that would carry people into an imaginary world," explain the architects, who developed the brand identity and experience through the architecture of the project. With the phrase *bota bota*, which means "drop by drop" in Japanese, they allude to the progressive immersion of visitors into a multisensory experience inspired by the aquatic environment, the maritime world, and the surrounding landscape. ~

HOUSEBOAT – *Lake Eildon, Victoria, Australia*
Built by Anchorage Houseboats, interior design by
Pipkorn & Kilpatrick, photography by Christine Francis

SERENE VIEWS AND MINIMALIST LUXURY

"The stunning natural backdrop of Lake Eildon and its surrounds was our inspiration for this unique project," note Melbourne-based interior designers Anna Pipkorn and Jane Kilpatrick. The duo was asked to cre-

ate the interior of a custom-made house-boat that would be used by a family of three generations on the lake in Victoria, Australia. Giving careful consideration to materials, colors, and the arrangement of the space, the designers set out to create calm and light-filled areas throughout the two-floor, 87 m² (936 ft.²) interior, which was completed in 2013. Integrated cabinetry ensures that "everything has its place, and every inch is utilized without it being obvious," while subtle natural textures add warmth. The division between public and private spaces receives unique expression on each level. »»

HOUSEBOAT – *Lake Eildon, Victoria, Australia*   42

"EVERYTHING HAS ITS PLACE, AND EVERY INCH IS UTILIZED WITHOUT IT BEING OBVIOUS."

» The upper level is more symmetrical in plan, with three bedrooms and a bathroom at one end and a combined kitchenette and lounge at the other. The ground level welcomes its inhabitants with great dynamics, as the master bedroom and bathroom are encircled by the "free flow of lounge, dining room, galley kitchen, and helm." ~

SCANDINAVIAN SPIRIT

Materials, colors, and the arrangement of the space were carefully considered in order to create calm and light-filled areas throughout the houseboat's two-floor interior.

WATERVILLA

In the Netherlands, +31 Architects are making their mark on the waterways with their impressive floating homes. Sleek and deceivingly simple, their luxurious "watervillas" are based on a rectangular concrete structure with a side of full-length windows atop a solid pontoon that adjusts to the rise and fall of the water as the tide changes. For the "Watervilla Weesperzijde" on Amsterdam's Amstel River, the clients wanted the main living area to merge with the water as much as possible. Large

sliding glass doors were placed on the water side for unobstructed views of the river from the kitchen and living room. The dark-framed panes are of nearly equal size, evoking a film strip that gives occasional glimpses of the residents within. "For the boats that are passing it looks as if a movie is played like a small intimate reality show," explain the architects. A full-length floating terrace seems to extend seamlessly from the interior space to increase interaction with the outside environment. The sense of floating and lightness continues with the open, floating staircase leading to the more private realm below. Here, natural light pours in through the »

» large window at the top of the stairs, augmented by cutaway walls and partial ceilings. On the quay side of the vessel, the aluminum façade is textured by a subtle pattern of holes that reveal the house number. At night, the holes are lit from behind for a futuristic look. ~

COPPER-CLAD "PARKARK"

A young family with a mooring in a park-land canal in Utrecht wanted "the full experience of living and floating on the water, though without the application of a hackneyed nautical form language,

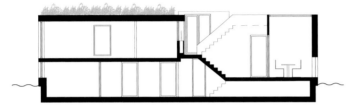

The living space is cleverly divided into multiple levels, with an open green roof that almost seems to be part of the surrounding park.

such as portholes," according to Richèl Lubbers of BYTR Architects. They wanted a home with privacy that would still grant a full view of the natural scenery. This balance was achieved through a carefully considered floor plan and clever fenestration for the three-level, three-bedroom dwelling. Glass doors and short staircases provide various access points and brighten up the open-plan living area. The decked terrace looks across the green roof down the canal and out into the surrounding landscape. The earthy tones of the exterior materials harmonize with the woodland and will weather gracefully over time. Part of the dwelling is tastefully textured with slats of environmentally friendly, thermally modified wood, while copper panels that reach the waterline gently blend the boat's façade with its reflection. ∼

PUBLIC PARK MEETS
PRIVATE OASIS

Copper panels and timber on the façade allow this stylishly functional home to blend in with its natural setting. Well-placed windows boast beautiful views of the scenery while allowing plenty of privacy.

FLOATING HOME – *Utrecht, Netherlands*

MINIMALIST LIVING

Once their daughter moved out to live on her own, Lisbeth Juul and Laust Nørgaard decided to return to living on water, which they had done for over a quarter of a century, save for a three year hiatus on land. "It's where our way of life is most fulfilled," says Juul. With a "less-is-more" concept for their new home, they aimed for "more sustainable and maintenance-free" living. For Juul and Nørgaard, a seasoned shipbuilder, the greatest challenge was not the structure but downsizing their lives to fit into an 80 m² (860 ft.²) abode—their smallest home yet. Floating on two concrete pontoons filled with lightweight polystyrene, the home took shape over eight months, and is now moored near the artificial island Ved Slusen, a quiet location 15 minutes from the city center. Its dark wood exterior contrasts with the natural clear varnished plywood lining the interior, which is paired with white walls for a clean, cabin-like feel. Full-length windows throughout the space establish an immediate connection to the water and bathe the rooms in natural light. "It's like living in a summerhouse all year round. The light is absolutely the most life-giving thing about it," says Juul. ~

A combination of plywood wall cladding and understated furnishings convey a sense of simple elegance. Large glass doors and windows provide plenty of natural light and an immediate connection to the water.

INDUSTRIAL SPIRIT

Enlisting the skills of architect Robert Nebolon, Kimo and Sarah Bertram decided to pursue a modern, "steel container" aesthetic inspired by their sur-

roundings for their three-level, 195 m² (2,100 ft²) floating home on Mission Creek in San Francisco. The blue and white metal siding and the saw-tooth roof recall the city's industrial past, while the front door and interior spiral staircase are painted in "International Orange," the color of the Golden Gate Bridge. Warehouse-style casement windows complete the look. A mix of modern and rustic furnishings made of natural materials and with color accents provide the interior with a warm feel. The layout makes the most commonly used areas light and bright. On the top level, windows that reach up to the high ceiling fill the open-plan living room and kitchen with sunlight. »»

The industrial-style structure radiates warmth thanks to an interior that tastefully unites modern and rustic colors, textures, and furnishings. Warehouse-style casement windows are tactfully integrated to bring in natural light wherever possible.

»» Bedrooms, bathrooms, and service areas are on the ground level. "The main challenge was determining how to pack the house with storage while ensuring it had the basics," said Nebolon. The bed in the master bedroom was built extra high to fit drawers underneath. Additional storage is available in the basement, which extends 1.5 m (5 ft.) below the waterline to accommodate a den and a third bedroom. ⁓

JAPANESE "WILDFLOWER" IN CALIFORNIA

A floating house built in the 1970s during the heyday of the eclectic houseboat community in Sausalito, California, displays a mix of

Island in the early '80s. According to a carpenter who worked on the project as a foreman, Kiddoo was commissioned by a Japanese-American businessman to build the private residence. While Kiddoo and his local team built most of the structure, the owner had a craftsman brought over with special materials from Japan for the third-floor interior, which features traditional sliding paper walls

Japanese tradition and American verve. The three-story, 325 m² (3,500 ft.²) floating home dubbed the "Wildflower" was built by master carpenter Forbes Thor Kiddoo, who made his fortune building Bay Area houseboats in the late '60s and '70s before creating his legendary Forbes

and custom tatami mats. In some cases, traditional Japanese joinery methods were employed, using no nails in the process. In its current incarnation, the owners have honored the original vision by combining elements from the original construction with contemporary furnishings. ~

Quirky found
objects add extra
flavor to this
eclectic mix of
Japanese
and American
craftsmanship.

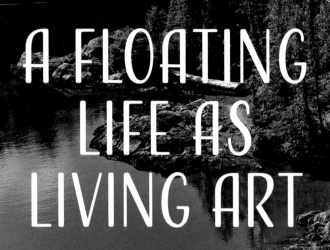

A FLOATING LIFE AS LIVING ART

FLOATING ISLAND – *Clayoquot Sound, Vancouver, Canada*
Owned & built by Catherine King & Wayne Adams

"THE BEAUTY OF FLOATING WAS THAT YOU COULD BE IN NATURE WITHOUT INTERFERING WITH IT."

For Catherine King and Wayne Adams, living "unplugged" in "Freedom Cove" is as much a way of life as a work of art: self-sufficient, devoted to creativity, and immersed in nature. For the past 25 years, they have lived on their floating complex in a remote coastal inlet of Cypress Bay near Tofino, on the west side of Vancouver Island in British Columbia, Canada. What Catherine experiences on a daily basis is a world far removed from that of landlubbing city dwellers: "I look out of my upstairs window and see moss green reflected in the water, bladderwrack kelp kissing the rocks on shore, and bright green sea lettuce caressing rocks peeking up through the water in the cove. It is low tide and the smell of salty sea is present, while in the background I hear crows cawing, seagulls squawking, and   »

» the constant yet comforting rat-a-tat-tat of the pileated woodpecker on a nearby cedar tree." When they met in 1987, Catherine and Wayne found in one another a kindred soul, both artists with a deep connection to nature and a keen interest in subsistence living. They first settled in the town of Tofino, where they planned on devoting their lives to their art—Wayne as a wildlife artist and carver, Catherine as a performing artist and healer. A fortuitous act of nature gave them the sign that it was time to act on their dream. While staying at a friend's cabin in Cypress Bay, a storm blew in a pile of lumbered

wood. Although they tried returning it to a nearby sawmill, the owner let them keep it. "We had already decided that we would build a float house to live in the wilderness at this point, after talking to other people who were floating. The beauty of floating was that you could be in nature without interfering with it," says King.

In the summer of 1991, Wayne used that lumber to build a small, floating house on the beach by the cabin they were staying in. Three months later it was ready, and in January 1992 they towed it by boat over to a protected cove they had discovered, naming their home »

GROW WITH THE FLOW

Catherine started with a small salad garden – and now manages half an acre of container garden as well as four greenhouses, where she grows vegetables, seasonal fruits, berries, herbs, and edible flowers.

LIVING "UNPLUGGED" IN "FREEDOM COVE" IS AS MUCH A WAY OF LIFE AS A WORK OF ART.

»» "Freedom Cove." Wayne designed and installed a gravity-fed fresh water system connected to a small cascade nearby. An outdoor dance platform was added for Catherine. Making a point of using recycled materials, they acquired an old fish farm system of styrofoam floats encased in hard plastic. This enabled them to add other floating platforms where Catherine started accumulating her garden. Over the years, their home has evolved to include the main house (twice as large as the original), two floating boat houses, a wood shed, a lighthouse with a washing machine and extra shower for guests, a power building for solar panels and batteries and two generators, a candle-making building, a gallery where they display their artwork, a smokehouse to smoke fish, and four greenhouses, where they grow their own fruits and vegetables. Their water and waste—they have two toilets, two showers, and a bathtub—flow   »»

» into a large tank that needs to be emptied only once a year. The complex is tied to the shore with large, weighted ropes in a spider web formation. This allows the whole system to move in one piece when hit with storms; the cove is protected from the Pacific Ocean's waves, but is subject to strong winds and rain. "The winter storms are the most challenging thing about living here. We learn from each one how to make the whole system stronger," explains Catherine. "We accept that the damage is part of the lifestyle and we use this damage as creative impetus to make change that is constructive and aesthetic. The entire system is really a big installation art piece that transforms every year." Although "Freedom Cove" feels remote, it is hardly cut off from the rest of the world. Every two weeks or so, Catherine and Wayne get staple foods in Tofino, roughly 10 miles away and a half-hour ride by boat. While their children were already grown when the couple moved alone to "Freedom Cove", their son later decided on a floating life and has his own floating home across the cove. They don't have phones, but since 2013 have Internet access. By opening their home to tours, says Catherine, they hope to "inspire others to follow their own dreams and to live in a manner that respects the earth and the environment." ~

BARGE LIFE FROM HOLLAND TO PARIS

"I wanted a cheap and unique place to live and a houseboat seemed like an interesting and exotic idea. I had no idea how hard it would be when I started out," says photojournalist and houseboat owner Zoriah Miller. When he purchased the Dutch barge built in 1930, it had no working sewage, electricity, heat, or navigation system, having been used as beachside tourist accommodation in Northern Holland for a decade before that. Whenever he was not working on an assignment abroad, Miller would fly to Holland and work on the boat. "It took me about two years to finish the basics and then I sailed through Holland, Belgium and eventually reached France, where I settled down outside of Paris," he says. Measuring 18 × 4.2 m (59 × 14 ft.), the boat blends contemporary comfort with historic accents.

The interior is divided into four main spaces: the kitchen, a breakfast nook that converts into a guest berth, living room, and main bedroom. It now has full amenities including a fully equipped kitchen with gas stove, a heated »

» bathroom floor, clothes washer and dryer. A thermostat-controlled wood pellet-burning stove, as well as an antique wood stove refitted to burn bioethanol provide extra heat, while its 31 windows, portholes, and skylights draw in plenty of natural light. ~

HOUSEBOAT – *Copenhagen, Denmark*
Owned by Jesper Holmberg Hansen & Jette Noa Liv Bøge

SHIPSHAPE DESIGN WITH SALVAGED MATERIALS

Jesper Holmberg Hansen and his part-ner Jette Noa Liv Bøge transformed a Dutch cargo boat into a two-level home for their family of four near an old shipyard and future creative hub in Copenhagen. Measuring 30 × 5 m (98.5 × 16.5 ft.) and dating back to the early 1900s, their barge is moored in a small houseboat community, just a 10-minute ferry ride to downtown. "We're surrounded by creative types like us, and we have the freedom to make our home the way we want it," says Jette, a former glassblower.

Additional rooms were built on deck with separate living quarters for guests and short-term rentals. Large windows and a glass floor bring sun-light into the space, and a green roof adds extra insulation. The interior echoes the warehouse setting, using materials sourced through Jesper's company Genbyg, a design studio and shop specializing in salvaged furni-ture, wood, and fixtures. Walls and floors rich in texture were pieced to-gether from reclaimed wood. A steel door from a military vessel found a   »»

»   second life in the bedroom, while an old scaffolding ladder leads up to a window seat. Vintage furniture merges thrifty chic with industrial flair. "The whole place is a testament to the power of recycling and the beauty of found objects," notes Jette. ~

The interior owes its unique flair to its eclectic collection of furniture—some picked up by Jette during her travels and at local flea markets and auctions, and some from Jesper's company Genbyg, which specializes in salvaged furniture, wood, and fixtures.

HOUSEBOAT – *Copenhagen, Denmark*

LIFE & WORK ABOARD THE "MARITOL"

Architect Olle Lundberg and his wife Mary Breuer transformed a decommissioned ferry from Iceland into a unique live/work space in San Francisco. "We were looking for more of a loft/commercial type space, but the tech boom had made those buildings unaffordable. So we decided to bring the space to San Francisco," he says.

lasted about 10 months—four in dry dock in Reykjavik and another six months in San Francisco. The electrical system was changed to an American one, and the plumbing overhauled. They set up a loft-like living room and bedroom on the main deck. A small kitchen for casual meals was installed on the open stern, separated from the

Measuring around 40 × 9.5 m (130 × 30 ft.) with four decks, "Tufjord" was built in 1975 and once carried passengers and cars through the Norwegian Sea. Under Lundberg's ownership it became "Maritol," the name a combination of his wife's first name and his initials. Renovations

living space by a large, glass-paned roll-up door. A large hole was cut in the deck to bring light into the dining room, kitchen, main bathroom, and guest berths on the lower level. After they sold the "Maritol" in 2011, it was re-purposed as a co-working space under the name the "Icebreaker." ~

The main deck serves as the central living area, while the galley one floor down holds a 9 m (30 ft.) cypress communal dining/work table, as well as Lundberg's impressive hot sauce collection.

FROM MID-CENTURY FERRY TO CREATIVE VILLA

Architect Nils Jeppe Hansen had dreamed of living on a houseboat ever since he was a child. This desire became so urgent that in 2000 he placed an ad in a trade magazine in search of a car ferry that could be converted into a houseboat. In 2001 Hansen became the proud owner of the "Fritz Juel," which had just carried its last load of cars that year. The transformation of the ferry, measuring about 34 × 10 m (110 × 33 ft.), into a houseboat was a labor of love, with Hansen committed to preserving as much of the original architecture as possible. On the deck where more than 20 cars were previously parked in three lanes, he inserted a long zinc-coated box with large floor-to-ceiling windows, providing a main living area measuring 20 meters (65 ft.) in length. Solar panels were added to the roof structure, which was raised so that it no longer touched the sides of the boat, but was connected to it by two bands of skylight windows. The engine was removed, providing more space in the hold for a total living area of around 350 m² (3767 ft.²). »»

CONVERTED FERRY – *Copenhagen, Denmark*   94

HANSEN COMMITTED TO PRESERVING AS MUCH OF THE ORIGINAL ARCHITECTURE AS POSSIBLE.

» The houseboat, nominated in 2012 as a finalist for "Denmark's Most Beautiful Home," maintains strong traces of its cultural heritage while offering a new mode of luxury living and working. Once the dream was ful-filled it was time to move on: in 2013 the "Fritz Juel" was sold to Danish celebrity jazz musician and television producer Thomas Blachman, who uses the vessel as his creative studio. ~

HE INSERTED A LONG ZINC-
COATED BOX WITH LARGE
FLOOR-TO-CEILING WINDOWS.

SUSTAINABLE CHIC

Portuguese nautical design and engineering firm, Friday, have come up with an energy-efficient, modular solution for living and working on water: the "FloatWing." With a fixed width of 6 m (20 ft.), it can vary in length between 10 m (33 ft.) and 18 m (59 ft.) for a variety of configurations from cozy studio to a three bedroom home. Built with materials such as plywood that have a low environmental impact, the "FloatWing" is available in various bedroom and bathroom configurations and customers can select from five different equipment levels. Thanks to its modular design, it can be packed into two standard shipping containers for easy transport. Sandwiched between two decks, the living area is surrounded almost entirely with floor-to-ceiling sliding glass panels. The most basic level is not motorized and relies on land connections for power and water. Higher levels add increasing autonomy, with solar panels and batteries, a pellet stove, tanks for fresh water and waste storage, and even a wastewater treatment system. While factors such as the available »

» amount of sunlight and the actual energy and water consumption of residents also come into play, the "FloatWing" can provide anywhere from seven days of standard energy self-sufficiency to six months, or even a year in its most experimental configuration. Mobility is provided by twin outboard motors reaching a top speed of three knots (3.5 mph / 5.6 km/h). As the designers explain, "the objective is not to move quickly, since the ride is part of the pleasure." ~

With a top speed of three knots, the "FloatWing" encourages its passengers to relish the experience of slow travel.

THE LIVING AREA IS SURROUNDED ALMOST ENTIRELY WITH FLOOR-TO-CEILING SLIDING GLASS PANELS.

103

CONVERTED FERRY – *Sluseholmen, Copenhagen, Denmark*
Designed by Birk Folke Daugaard & Michael Daugaard

FROM FERRY TO FLOATING HOME

"I was at the local watchmaker to change my watch battery. A beautiful maritime watch was on the counter, and I mentioned that it would be nice to live on the water. 'Then I have a project for you,' said the watchmaker. 'It's a ferry full of love and it's up for sale.' This sentence sparked my idea to make the old 'Skansehage' ferry my home," explains Michael Daugaard. The old oak wood vessel built in 1959 transported happy summer travelers and their cars between Rørvig and Hundested for around 50 years. Two years after buying it, Daugaard and his partner Karen Løth Sass moved into a beautiful custom houseboat. Daugaard's son, architect Birk Folke Daugaard, redesigned the space with reclaimed materials for a cozy and personal atmosphere. "Nothing here is straight or minimalistic," reassures Sass. The windows, for example, date back to the 1940s. Today, the "Skansehage" is docked in Sluseholmen, which has a unique ⟫⟫

"IT'S A FERRY FULL OF LOVE AND IT'S UP FOR SALE."

»» colony of 10 houseboats that were all converted from retired work boats. Measuring 30 × 7.5 m (98 × 25 ft.), it has a spacious ground floor with an open lounge and kitchen, and two outdoor terraces. Below deck are the master bedroom, a guest room, a bathroom, and storage. ~

HOUSEBOAT – *Amsterdam, Netherlands*
Designed by Hoyt Architects

A FAMILY AFFAIR

A family in Amsterdam in search of a houseboat fell in love with an old Belgian river barge, whose spacious cargo hold presented great potential.

"Because the cargo hold measures 5 × 30 m (16.4 × 98.4 ft.) and is 3.2 m (10.4 ft.) high, it was possible to fit the program of a very spacious apartment or even a suburban row house, something quite unique for the Amsterdam city center," explain Hoyt Architects in Rotterdam. As the hold of a freight barge tends to be dark and gloomy, their main aim was to transform it into an airy living space. The steel interior was insulated and covered with light-colored plywood. A cement floor was cast on top of the insulation and piping. To draw in natural light, 18 oversized bronze portholes were »

At one end of the barge, the deckhouse and steering hut were restored and modernized, and can be rented out as an independent mini-apartment.

》 cut into the hull, a patio was introduced, and skylights added. The interior, completed in 2013, was designed in close collaboration with the clients, reflecting their artistic background and restaurant experience—a central element is the cooking island in the large, open kitchen. The patio connects the common living area with the private quarters and creates a corridor that leads to the parents' room, bathroom, and children's bedroom. ～

HOUSEBOAT – *Amsterdam, Netherlands* 114

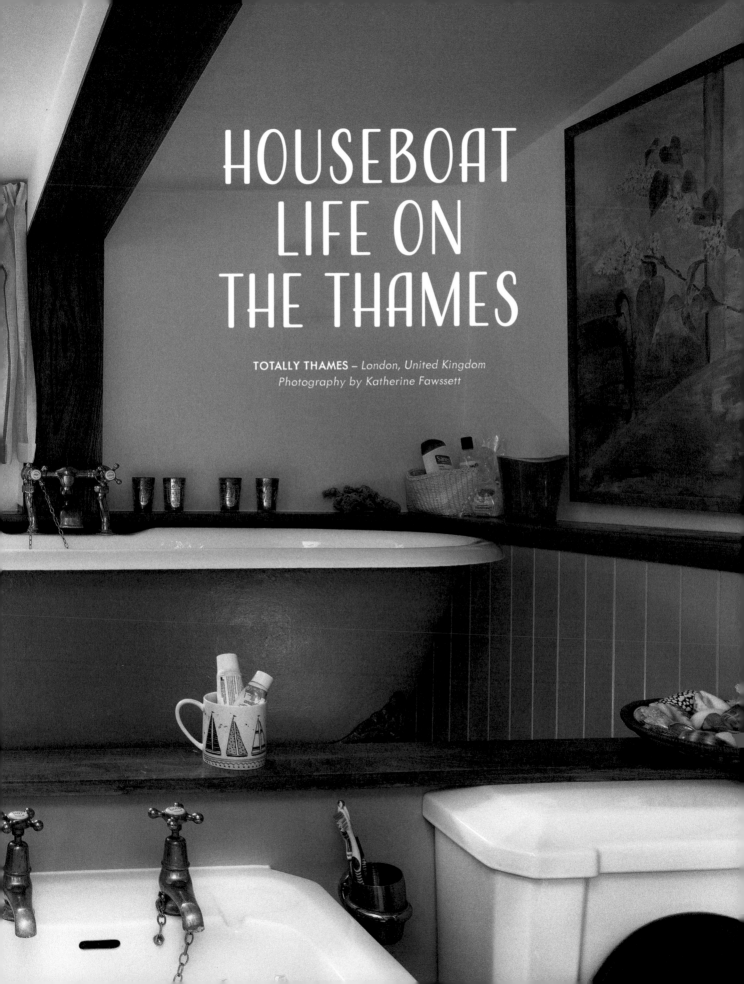

HOUSEBOAT LIFE ON THE THAMES

TOTALLY THAMES – *London, United Kingdom*
Photography by Katherine Fawssett

LIVEABOARD LUXURY

Adventurous explorers can go island hopping through the remote Indonesian archipelago while living in luxury aboard a modern phinisi, a traditional Indonesian twin-masted wood schooner

based on the nineteenth century vessels crafted by the Bugis seafarers from south Sulawesi. A growing number of high-end hotel groups and individual enterprises are offering elite access to pristine beaches, crystal clear waters, and the amazing biodiversity found among the many small islands that have remained untouched by mass tourism. The "Alila Purnama," owned by the Alila luxury group, is a prime example. Measuring 46 m (150 ft.) from bow to stern, the "Purnama" hosts up to 10 guests in five elegant ensuite cabins across three decks. The furniture throughout the ship is custom-made from teak, rattan, and other locally sourced materials. »»

»   A dedicated crew of 16, including a dive master, excursion guide, spa therapist, and master chef, caters to every need. Boarding the "Purnama" in Labuan Bajo on the island of Flores, guests can charter the entire boat for a customized excursion or book a spot on one of the seasonal expeditions to Komodo Island, Cenderawasih Bay, or Raja Ampat. ~

FLOATING HOTEL – *Island of Flores, Labuan Bajo, Indonesia*   132

The "Purnama" anchoring in a bay at the Komodo islands.

MOSCOW MODULAR

"I often think about modular architecture and wonder where the limits are. Are climate or nature a restriction? How much space do people need to be comfortable?" Architect Ivan

Ovchinniko addresses these issues and more with DD16, the newest addition to his DublDom range of prefab homes. The ultra-compact structure is designed for factory production, quick and easy transport, and installation in extreme conditions, such as in the mountains or on water—all while maximizing comfort and affordability.

DD16 has an interior space of just 16 m² (172 ft.²) sleeping up to three people, plus a veranda of 7 m² (75 ft.²). Milled ports in its engineered wood frame decrease weight and reduce cold bridges. High-performance polyurethane foam serves as insulation. The aluminum cladding is lightweight and robust. Indoor elements have hidden storage, multiple uses, or can be fully folded away.   »»

Full-length mirror glazing opens up the space while maintaining privacy. Installed on a lake near Moscow, the DD16 pictured here rests on modular pontoons that were transported with the unit and quickly assembled on site. It uses autonomous systems such as solar panels for electricity, water from the lake, and a bio toilet.

Despite being close to the city, "it feels like you are on a wild river somewhere in a forest thicket," says Ovchinnikov. "The house turns with the wind, so the view is constantly changing." ~

BELOW SEA LEVEL

Just a few minutes' boat ride from the shore of Pemba Island in Tanzania's Zanzibar Archipelago is the Manta Resort's "Underwater Room," an exclusive three-level hotel suite floating in the crystal clear waters of the Indian Ocean. The floating structure, clad in local hardwood, was designed by Swedish artist Mikael Genberg, who constructed a similar structure in Sweden's Lake Mälaren. Here, the "Underwater Room" is located in a "blue hole," a deep, circular clearing within the coral reef measuring about 50 m (164 ft.) in diameter and teeming with marine life. Attached to the ocean floor by four anchors, the structure sways with the movement of the waves. Squid, jellyfish,

and shoals of reef fish are drawn to the room and illuminated by spotlights above and below the room's eight windows for a mesmerizing panoramic view. Above water, guests can take in the sunset as they dine on the sea-level deck, or use the bathroom facilities, which include an open-air fresh water shower and an eco-friendly marine toilet. A ladder leads to the rooftop deck for sunbathing and sleeping beneath the stars. ∼

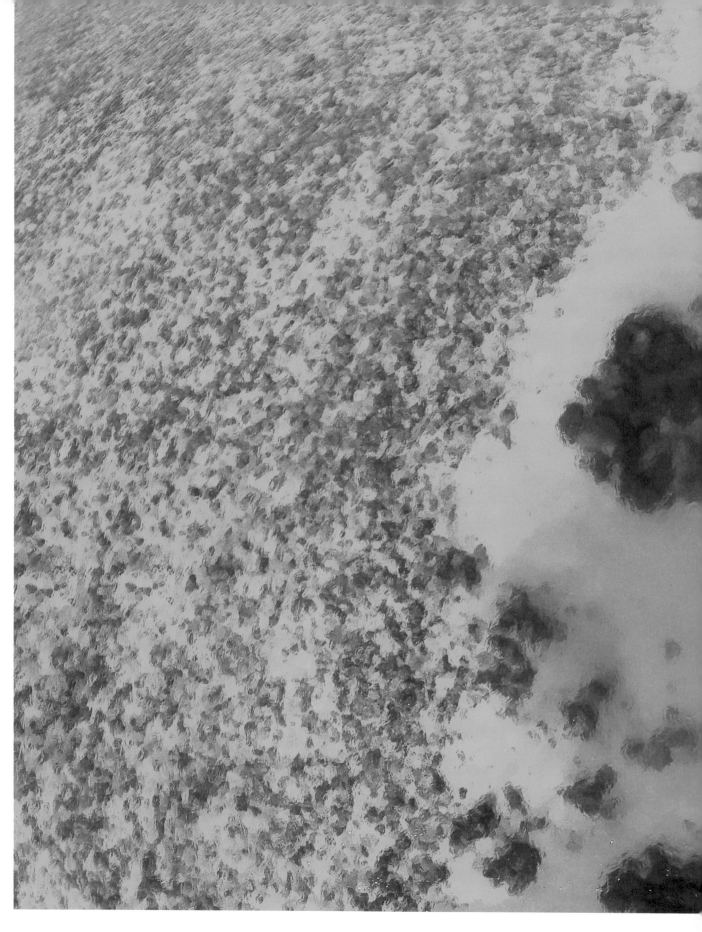

FLOATING HOTEL SUITE – *Pemba Island, Tanzania*   142

AMPHIBIOUS ARCHITECTURE

Urban mobility takes on new dimensions in the "Rolling and Floating Masterplan" developed by Stockholm-based Jägnefält Milton architects in 2010. Their proposal for the Norwegian port town of Åndalsnes reactivates its old industrial railroad tracks to establish a new, flexible infrastructure. Mobile modular structures can be moved and rearranged throughout the urban space according to the seasons and situations in order to stage events such as festivals, concerts, and markets. The master plan

includes examples of a rolling hotel, a public bath, and a concert hall, whose variable locations and configurations offer the potential for a lively and dynamic landscape. The use of small-scale amphibious modules would enable »

Public and private amphibious units can be rolled out along train tracks as needed, and mixed and matched according to season and event.

»   the city to expand in response to fluctuations in tourism while keeping costs down, and reinforce the connection between the land and water. To solve the need for electricity, water, and waste treatment, the architects proposed the installation of a pipeline along the tracks, allowing the buildings to plug into services as required. ~

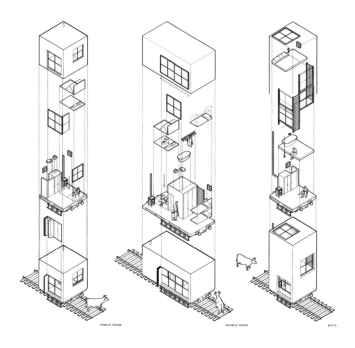

SINGLE ROOM   DOUBLE ROOM   SUITE

147

THE EXBURY EGG

For 12 months, artist Stephen Turner lived alone in a compact floating structure called the "Exbury Egg" in the Beaulieu Estuary in southern England. During this sojourn, he examined the changing patterns of the marine ecology while making artworks inspired, influenced, and informed by his surroundings. The project was led by art, architecture, and education consultants Space Placemaking and Urban Design (SPUD Group). Measuring approximately 6 × 2.8 m (19.6 × 9 ft.), the "Egg" was created and designed by PAD studio and Stephen Turner. It was built by local boat builder Paul Baker, using traditional techniques and locally sourced timber. "My contribution to the design concept of the structure was its symbolic egg form, that will decay and change during my occupation; turning the egg into a calendar revealing the impact of 365 days of changing weather and tides upon its surface," says Turner. "If the 'Exbury Egg' symbolizes fertility, birth, and renewal, it is, equally, a reminder of our difficult relationship with nature and of the heavy footprints that mark our path as we bestride the planet." An ongoing record of Turner's work with the "Egg" can be seen on the project website. ~

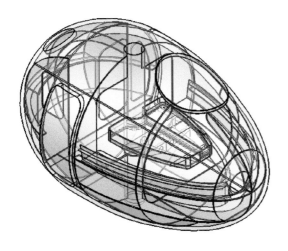

"ITS SYMBOLIC EGG FORM
WILL DECAY AND CHANGE
DURING MY OCCUPATION."

FLOATING FINNISH SAUNA

Saunas are an integral part of Finnish culture, so it made sense that when a group of friends decided to build a place for get-togethers on the Pielisjoki River in Joensuu, Finland, it would naturally include a sauna. Built from reclaimed wood, their multilevel raft, dubbed the "Saunalautta" (Finnish for

"sauna-raft"), is part sauna, and part houseboat or mobile campsite. Measuring 3.20 × 7.50 m (10.5 × 25 ft.), it floats on 12 small pontoons, and is powered by a small outboard motor. Inside is a cozy sauna that fits 10 to 15 people, and a berth that sleeps up to five. The two outdoor decks offer plenty of room for relaxation, with a BBQ and dining table on the upper deck and hammocks all around. Six meters (19 ft.) up is a crow's nest overlook that doubles as a diving tower for the brave of heart. The owners have decided to share their fun by making the "Saunalautta" available for short-term rent. ～

HOLIDAY VILLAGE IN FRANCE

For a new way to reconnect with nature, the "Village Flottant (Floating Village) de Pressac" in southwestern France offers 20 off-grid cabins floating on an idyllic lake. Accessible by row boat or via a bridge from the bank, the cozy cabins are available and trout from the deck of their private cabin. Although the cabins do not have cooking facilities, a floating dining room offers the opportunity to prepare your catch of the day on a barbecue. Breakfast, as well as optional lunch and dinner, are delivered by boat.

in different sizes, sleeping up to five people. Made from oak, larch, and Douglas fir sourced from European forests, the dwellings include a sawdust toilet, a small water tank for simple washing, and solar powered lights. The six-hectare natural lake where the resort is located, L'Etang du Ponteil, is a delight for fishing enthusiasts, who can catch carp, pike, Showers, flushing toilets, a swimming pool, restaurant, and nature center are all located close by on land. According to the resort manager Laurent Debiais, the idea behind this unique concept was to "allow guests to discover the pleasure of relaxing in a beautiful site and to reconnect with wildlife and each other, away from the pressures and stresses of everyday life." ∼

FLOATING DOMES
ON SLOVENIAN LAKE

Visitors to Lake Velenje in Slovenia might catch a glimpse of the fantastic "Floating City." The floating complex of geodesic domes is the brainchild of Elvis Halilović, co-founder of ONDU, a design studio also known for its wooden pinhole cameras. After building a series of geodesic domes on land for both private and commercial use, Halilović took the idea to the water. As he explains, the "'Floating City' was designed to be a modular platform, made for testing technologies and aspects of self-sufficient living. The object is designed and made in such a way that it has no unwanted impact on the surrounding environment." Together with his father, brother, and a friend, Halilović built four lightweight timber and polycarbonate domes, measuring 5 m (16.4 ft.) across and held together   »»

»   by high-quality wood screws.
These were then mounted on a floating grid of wooden beams and recycled plastic drums. Although the goal
of making the floating city a fully
self-sufficient, off-grid artist retreat
was ultimately not fulfilled, it remains
intact and floating on the lake even
five years after its construction "with
more or less no maintenance." It is
often visited by the many kayakers,
stand up paddle boarders, and
canoers who frequent the lake. ~

RAFT STRUCTURE – *Velenje Lake, Slovenia*

FLOATING SAUNA – *Seattle, Washington, USA*
Designed by goCstudio

CROWDFUNDED PUBLIC SAUNA

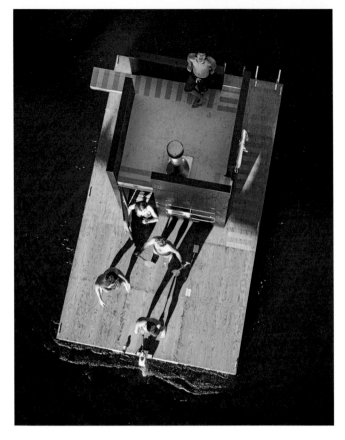

Capturing the spirit of "small project, big impact," young Seattle-based design studio goCstudio created "wa_sauna," a floating sauna for community use on the city's lakes. "The idea for the floating sauna was born on a cold and wet winter's day. We were searching for a way to engage the water surrounding our city, enticing visitors onto the lakes year 'round," explain the architects. The compact, spruce lined sauna is 4 m (14 ft.) high and fits up to six people. Its 22 m² (240 ft.²) plywood platform lets visitors lounge in the sun or dive into the crisp waters of Seattle's lakes, while a low-speed battery-powered trolling motor moves the sauna from one location to the next. The project was funded through the support of the local community and a crowdfunding campaign in the fall of 2014, raising over $40,000. In the same spirit, it was built by the studio together with a team of skilled volunteers. Towing the two-ton (4,500 lb) structure eight blocks from its building site to a boat ramp and into the water was a challenging process that took almost three hours. As the architects recall, "The contrast of steel casters on rough gravel and pavement to the feeling of this structure gently floating was the most exciting moment of the build process." ~

TOWABLE CAMPER TRANSFORMS INTO MINI-BOAT

Glampers looking to indulge in leisurely outdoor activities on both land and water will appreciate the flexibility of the amphibious "Sealander." This "mobile leisure housing" solution designed by Daniel Straub in Kiel, Germany, and first seen in 2014, doubles as a snug camping trailer and a fully functional compact houseboat. Measuring about 4 × 1.7 m (13 × 5.6 ft.), the six-person vessel is formed from a single piece of fiberglass-reinforced plastic, a material that is both lightweight and robust. Panorama windows and a convertible roof allow for plentiful light and enjoyable views. The two bench seats convert into a bed for two adults and a child. The 5-hp electric outboard motor is suitable for cruising in calm and shallow water at around 8.8 km/h (5.5 mph). Units can be customized with additional features, such as cooking and wash modules, a toilet, shower, on-board barbecue, and an audio system for maximum convenience and pleasure. The vessel's appearance can also be tailored, from the exterior paint to colors for upholstery, curtains, and the folding top, as well as the interior wood paneling. ~

PANORAMA WINDOWS AND A CONVERTIBLE ROOF ALLOW FOR PLENTIFUL LIGHT AND ENJOYABLE VIEWS.

Drive to the lake
and roll right into
the water with the
Sealander, which
serves as your own
private island,
excursion boat,
and resting place
rolled into one.
You don't even need
a boating license
to operate it.

A MODEL'S WHIM

When model and designer Kyleigh Kühn moved back to the Bay Area with her boyfriend, from New York, instead of getting a high-priced apartment, she de-

cided to invest in a houseboat that would be all their own. She impulsively bought a low-priced, run-down 1979 Gibson houseboat. "The boat's name was 'Whim,' which seemed perfect," says Kühn. Over 18 months, Kühn and her boyfriend restored and redesigned the boat to make the most of its 40 m² (432 ft.²) living area. The fiberglass hull was renewed and the original dark wood-paneled interior gutted. Thanks to the efficient use of space and thoughtful furnishings, the new space is cozy and light. By lofting the bed, they created additional space for a lounge area and a built-in desk below it. Drawers and cubbyholes were added under the stairs for extra storage space. The view from the bed opens onto the expanded kitchen, which includes a full-size porcelain sink, butcher block counters, and a two-burner electric range. Handmade driftwood shelves and elegant brass accents reference the nautical theme of the surrounding landscape. The result is a beautiful home—now in search of a new owner, as Kühn moves onto her next project. ~

HANDMADE DRIFTWOOD
SHELVES AND ELEGANT
BRASS ACCENTS REFERENCE
A NAUTICAL THEME.

HOUSEBOAT – *Sausalito, California, USA*

PÉNICHE WITH PANACHE

Finding the perfect houseboat for canal living in the heart of Amsterdam was no easy task for this family of four. Houseboats there can be no more than 5 × 25 m (16.5 × 82 ft.) in size, but the historic French *péniche* (motorized cargo barge) they had fallen in love with was a standard 38 × 5.05 m (125 × 16.6 ft.). Ultimately, they opted for a custom build with classic flair.

Getting the plans approved by the authorities was a back-and-forth process lasting about one-and-a-half years—but the wait was worth it. The outside has a vintage feel with its wood wheelhouse, bull's-eye windows, colorful trim, and cozy terrace. But the 140 m² (1,500 ft.²) interior is decidedly contemporary. A kitchen counter along the length of the wall in the main living area maximizes space, while a seating platform adds a sense of dynamics. A home cinema console hides cables and equipment and doubles as a dividing wall. Built-in storage keeps clutter at bay. Despite the convenience of living in the city center, there are also challenges. During special events, crowds pack the canals, which has led to damage to the houseboat in the past. "We now have donut-like bumpers hanging all around it. And we hire two or three security men. Nowadays we protect our boat like a fortress." ~

DEN HOLLANDER
794 S

MULTI-LEVEL FAMILY ABODE

Over the course of nine months, Bas van Schelven and Wendy Rommers transformed a freight barge from the 1930s into a modern family houseboat. Originally 50 m (164 ft.) long, the barge was shortened to 34 m (112 ft.) due to the restrictions of their berth in Zaandam, a small city on the outskirts of Amsterdam. The vessel's interior width of 6.6 m (21.6 ft.) gave them plenty of floor space, which they enhanced by creating a loft-like ambience—not a problem for the trained architect and his partner, who is a graphic and interior designer. The old skipper's quarters at the front of the boat were converted into a guest room, bathroom, and children's bedroom with two sleeping niches. Higher up, the wheelhouse offers a panoramic view of the surroundings. Descending another staircase leads to the kitchen and terrace. On the level below that, are the living room, laundry room, two more bedrooms, and a bathroom with sauna. "Jolie," as they have named their new home, is fully operational as a boat and also sustainable. Rooftop solar panels provide the energy needed for hot water and heat from March to October. In winter, a wood-burning stove generates additional warmth. ～

ROOFTOP SOLAR PANELS
PROVIDE THE ENERGY NEEDED
FOR HOT WATER AND HEAT.

HOUSEBOAT – *Zaandam, Netherlands*

HORTICULTURE ON THE HUDSON

Should food be a basic human right? "Swale," a floating food forest and experiential artwork founded in 2016 by artist Mary Mattingly in New York City, aims to spark debate about this question and more. Now in its second year, "Swale" has docked at various public piers in Manhattan, Brooklyn, and Governors Island. The project is constructed on a 12 × 40 m

(40 × 130 ft.) flat deck barge, and features an edible forest garden that uses rainwater and purified river water. The design is structured as a floating island for community activities and artistic events, as well as a wide range of eco-initiatives. During public hours, when "Swale" is open free of charge, visitors are encouraged to pick fresh produce, including apples, various berries, and herbs. Although "Swale's" future depends on adequate funding, it has already made an impact on urban policy, notes Mattingly: "As a direct »»

>> result of 'Swale' and the support of community groups, the New York City Department of Parks and Recreation will pilot the first public 'food way' in NYC in Concrete Plant Park. Concrete Plant Park is a 24-hour greenway that will contain edible perennial plantings for anyone to forage from." ~

FLOATING GARDEN – *New York City, USA*

SWIMMING CITIES
OF
SERENISSIMA

FLOATING RAFTS – *Adriatic Sea*
Created by Swoon & Friends

Equal parts sculpture, performance, and social experiment, the "Swimming Cities of Serenissima"—the brainchild of Brooklyn-based artist Caledonia Curry, aka Swoon—consisted of three rafts hand-crafted from salvaged materials by an on-board crew of 30 artists, which navigated the Adriatic Sea from the port city of Koper, Slovenia, to Venice in May 2009.

The project built on two previous collaborative floating art projects by Swoon and her cohorts. In the summers of 2006 and 2007, the "Miss Rockaway Armada" traveled down the Mississippi River from Minneapolis to New Orleans on three scrap-crafted rafts, treating onlookers to live performances along the way. For the "Swimming Cities of Switchback

Sea" in 2008, seven such performing rafts floated for three weeks down the Hudson River from upstate New York to New York City. The "Swimming Cities of Serenissima" traveled to the source of inspiration for Swoon's raft projects, taking its name from one of the many monikers of the northeastern Italian city built on wooden platforms in a lagoon off the Adriatic Sea. »»

» "I knew from the first time I entered the city of Venice by water that I would make an artwork that was a kind of interactive homage to the place. I also knew I wanted the trip to be a journey. Slovenia seemed a natural starting place, especially the Karst region, which was where the timbers that built the pilots of Venice originated."

Building materials for two of the rafts, reused from the previous projects, were flown to Slovenia; a third was made from materials scavenged on location. After a multi-week construction process integrating items such as pickle barrels, shipping styrofoam, and dresser drawers, "Alice," "Maria," and "Old Hickory" cast off, powered by modified Mercedes car engines with long-tail propellers. "Each raft had a unique design for steering, so piloting them was very different depending on the boat, and often required more than one person," notes photographer Tod Seelie, whose extensive boating experience came in handy during the ambitious project. The journey took nearly a month, as the team

stopped to camp and collect things for their floating "cabinet of wonders"—as Swoon describes it—which "became a morbid reliquary of dead things we found along the way … lots of bones and feathers and pelts, some lovely found objects, some art." Aside from the basic inconveniences of riding on a bare-bones raft (without a

toilet) for weeks on end, a serious challenge faced by the crew was the sudden storm that blew down from the mountains, called the Bora. As Seelie recalls, "Our vessels had very low freeboard, and we would often have water wash across the deck in even low chop, so a big storm posed a very serious threat." But the greatest challenge was navigating the bureaucracy once they got to the Venetian coastline. "Venice has its own maritime law," explains Swoon. "In Italy and Slovenia, they were like look, we would never have let you do this, but international maritime law says that we respect the boating laws of the country that your boats are »

PORTIONS OF THE RAFTS CAME ALIVE WITH MUSIC AND PUPPETRY.

»»   registered in, and it was easy for us to find loopholes in the laws of the U.S. But when we got to Venice they were like, oh hell no, we have laws way older than that, and you're gonna listen to us. We found some ways around, but it was a whole other level of challenge than just dealing with the U.S. Coast Guard."

Using nearby Certosa Island as their base, they would dock in various places along the edge of the city, tying the rafts together like a big barge. As people watched from the street, portions of the rafts came alive with music and puppetry, like a traditional cuckoo clock, recounts Seelie. "After the performance, we would welcome people onto the rafts, and if they stuck around long enough, give them a ride on our way back to our island home."

For the tight-knit crew, a major highlight was penetrating the heart of Venice, cruising down the Grand Canal despite all the red tape. "We had been denied permission to enter the canal multiple times, but we did it anyway under the cover of night, and risked going to jail," says Seelie. "The band Dark Dark Dark was playing live on one of the rafts, so there was this spooky melodic soundtrack to our voyage down the middle of an ancient piece of history. It was a bit like stepping into a sliver of magical realism." ~

SECOND LIFE FOR A LIFEBOAT

For Simon White in England, the decision to live in a houseboat was a way to achieve a better work-life balance. "I realized that I don't want to work full time until I retire to then die. I'd rather live more now and work a little bit less," he says. The £2,000 per year he pays for a mooring on the Avon River near Bristol is a significant saving over the £9,500 he previously paid to rent a flat in nearby Bath. In 2016, over the course of six months, he spent around £16,000 to convert an old lifeboat into a cozy off-grid abode. With a maximum capacity of 56 people, the boat, 9.7 × 3.6 m (31.8 × 11.8 ft.), had been used during the 1980s on an oil rig in the North Sea. Today, the boat has running water and electricity, solar panels, a wet room with

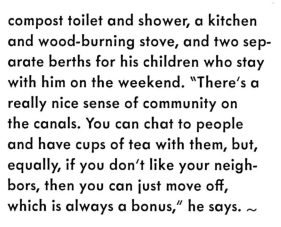

compost toilet and shower, a kitchen
and wood-burning stove, and two separate berths for his children who stay
with him on the weekend. "There's a
really nice sense of community on
the canals. You can chat to people
and have cups of tea with them, but,
equally, if you don't like your neighbors, then you can just move off,
which is always a bonus," he says. ~

DIY TIMBER RAFT

For a completely off-grid adventure holiday, head for Värmland County near the border of Norway. The company Vildmark i Värmland offers visitors the opportunity to build their own timber rafts and float down the clear waters of Klarälven River, the longest river in Sweden. Where logs were floated down the river to supply the paper industry until 1991, nature lovers can now drift along at a leisurely average of one to two knots per hour, taking in the flora and fauna of the bucolic landscape. Founded in 1980, the company offers couples and groups different timber rafting packages ranging from one to eight days. The first day is spent learning by doing, building your own traditional timber raft using logs and ropes, and practicing how to steer, maneuver out of tricky situations like sandbanks and

eddies, and how to get to land again. Travelers camp in tents or cabins along the river or sleep on their docked raft. The experience is "an excellent opportunity for teamwork in the family or with your friends," says co-owner Anders Junler, who has been with the company since the nineties. ~

YANKEE SPIRIT LIVES ON

CONVERTED FERRY – *New York City, USA*
Owned by Richard & Victoria MacKenzie-Childs

Call it luck or even destiny—when renowned artists Richard and Victoria MacKenzie-Childs discovered the "Yankee Ferry," it marked the start of yet another fascinating chapter in its already long and colorful history.

Built in 1907 in Philadelphia, the vessel started out as a passenger ferry in Maine's Calendar Islands and in Boston Harbor. When the United States joined World War I in 1917, it was conscripted to move troops and supplies. In 1921, it brought newly arriving immigrants to Manhattan to start new lives—today it is the last and oldest existing Ellis Island Ferry. At the end of the decade, it returned to moving commercial passengers around New York and then Rhode Island, before being summoned for military duty in the 1940s during World War II. After the war, it again ferried commercial passengers for nearly 40 years until its retirement in 1983. A private collector saved it from the scrapyard in 1990, towed it to New York City for restoration, and had it listed as a National Historic Place. Enter the MacKenzie-Childs. »»

In search of a new studio in New York City at the end of the nineties, the artists were unable to find a suitable space for a reasonable price. Victoria had an idea: "I thought, hey, if we can't afford to live and work and produce on land, then let's have our studio be on the water."

In 2003 they purchased the "Yankee Ferry," which has been a work-in-progress ever since. Docking around New York City, the creative couple has spent the years revivifying the four-deck, 45-m-long (147 ft.) vessel with their signature whimsical style. It has served as their home and studio, showcasing products from their home décor business in situ. Victoria points out that as artists they see the Yankee primarily as a place of creation—the focus is not on the houseboat lifestyle. "Lifestyle is how the world sees it. I've never been interested in a lifestyle; we're workers. We work to express and to overcome challenges. And necessity is the mother of invention. The beauty comes out of our »

Earnings from the Yankee's "Sleepaboard" program went towards a waste-water and sewage treatment system, as well as fun and surprising features such as a hanging dining table that can be hoisted out of the way by a pulley system.

THEIR OVERHAUL OF THE INTERIOR INCLUDED SEVERAL BEDROOMS SLEEPING UP TO 20 PEOPLE.

»   natural, almost folkloric sculpture and art. Our eye just naturally finds a way to order things." From the beginning, the MacKenzie-Childs have recognized in the "Yankee Ferry," with its illustrious history, great potential as a catalyst for change, as a place where people from around the world can come together and develop new ideas and perspectives. To this end, their overhaul of the interior included several bedrooms sleeping up to 20 people and a large communal dining room that converts into a ballroom able to fit 150 people. Through an unofficial stay-aboard program, or "sleepeasy," they rented out rooms to international visitors, hosted private and public events, photo shoots, class trips, and business brainstorming sessions. All of the proceeds were funneled back into the care of this total work of art that is maintained by the MacKenzie-Childs, their dedicated boatswain Frederick, and an enthusiastic temporary crew.

As of this writing, the "Yankee" is undergoing routine repairs in dry dock on Staten Island, while its owners explore possibilities for a new location, and possibly finding new owners for the vessel. "Above all," says Victoria, "We're hoping for her to be in her rightful place, where she can serve the community and change the world." ∼

CONSTANT CRUISING ALONG THE CANALS

Theo, a filmmaker and photographer, and Bee, an animal conservationist and writer, left their 9-to-5 lifestyle in Birmingham to go on the road and

off-grid, living for two years out of a converted Volkswagen Transporter. Under the name "The Indie Projects," they documented their life on social media while traveling across Europe. Now the couple has embarked on the next chapter of their project: exploring Britain's canal network aboard Bertha, a 9 m (30 ft.) 1991 Springer Cruiser. Fans can see their extensive renovation of the vessel, and learn how living on a narrowboat in contrast to "#vanlife" offers a different tempo of living and the added luxury of a shower, a proper kitchen, and more personal space. "With laptops, we have the freedom to move around the boat and chill on our bed or comfy chairs, or even the roof if the weather is decent," says Bee. Since staying   »»

»» connected to the online community is integral to their project, a main concern was internet access, which they manage through their mobile phones. "It's not like in our van, where we could park outside a McDonald's and pick up their Wi-Fi; here we are completely remote." ~

A NARROWBOAT
IN LONDON

NARROWBOAT – *London, United Kingdom*
Owned by Retts Wood

For London-based photographer Retts Wood, moving from land onto a houseboat was a matter of everything coming together at the right time. "I had come out of a long relationship when a friend bought a boat and invited a few of us to join him on his first cruise, from the outskirts of London into town. I fell in love with the whole thing instantly and started making plans that night. It just seemed like the perfect life for me—small and sweet and affordable, in the most expensive of cities,"　»

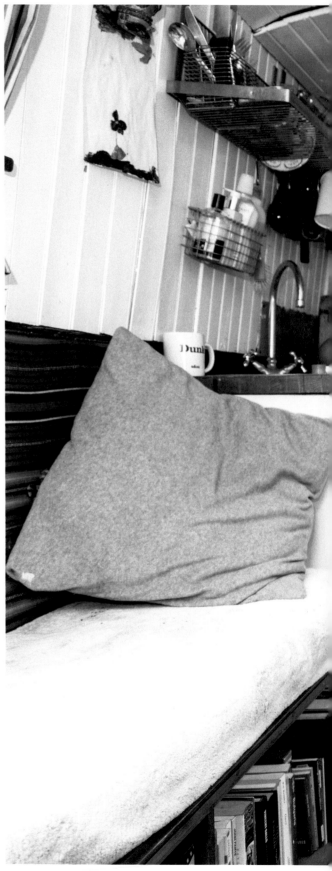

»   says Wood. After discovering a used narrowboat on a boat sales website, she went to view it in nearby Oxford, made an offer on the spot, and returned a week later to get the keys. "Then I set off down the Thames, never having been alone on a boat before. Luckily, Thames lock keepers are some of the kindest and most helpful people you could wish to meet."

Shortly afterwards, Wood went to Brazil, still trying to think of a name for her new acquisition. There she was given the nickname *borboleta* which means "butterfly" in Portuguese, for the butterfly tattoo on her arm. Back in London, she realized it would be the perfect name for her new floating home.

The key distinguishing feature of a narrowboat is its width, which must be less than 2.13 m (7 ft.), to navigate the British canals. "Borboleta" is on the smaller side, measuring about 1.8 × 11.6 m (6 × 38 ft.), so that it could turn around in wider areas of the canal, and was easy to moor. Working as a freelance photographer gave Wood the time to renovate the boat's interior   »

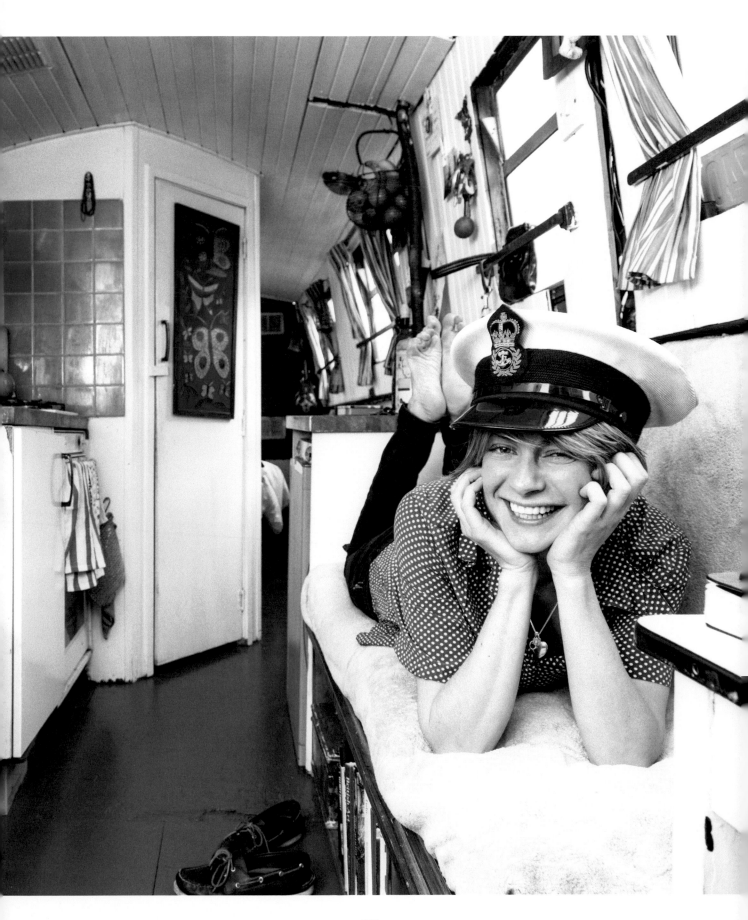

"I DON'T IMAGINE MOST PEOPLE MOVE INTO HOUSES AND RIP EVERYTHING OUT."

»»   herself. "A boat-owning friend advised me that you can change anything inside but you need a good hull and a good engine. I followed that advice, but did completely rip out the inside and start again, which was challenging but wonderful too. I don't imagine most people move into houses and rip everything out and rebuild more or less single-handedly, but a boat is small enough that it seems not only possible but also easier."

Inside, the narrow space begins at the bow with a wood- and coal-burning stove for heat, two benches that convert into a bed, followed by a kitchen area, then a bathroom (with a small bathtub) as a separate room, creating a corridor on one side leading to the main berth at the stern.

Wood initially worked from home—while photo shoots were on location, she did the editing on her laptop—but this soon proved to be   »»

»   impractical, so she moved her work to a studio on land. "I was not connected to mains electricity so I was running my computer and scanner off the 12-volt leisure battery, and I didn't have enough storage for all my negatives and so on. Also, my boat felt like such a cozy little womb I preferred to keep my work outside of it."

For 10 years, Wood lived on the boat in the Thames, cruising along the open river in summer and hunkered down amid an eclectic community of narrowboat owners on the canal in winter. "I love the canal's perfect balance of wild nature and heavy industry. My boat neighbors were a wide-ranging bunch but some of the most wonderful people I've ever come across," she recalls.

Ultimately, she left her life afloat due to size constraints and the logistics that come with having two children. When her first son was born, she simply converted the desk next to   »

» her bed into a baby cot and moved some of her clothes out of a drawer to make room for his. "The boat was the best place to be with him. He was always close by, even if we were at opposite ends. When he was teething, I'd take him outside, as the night air calmed him down." But the space wasn't big enough to hold a second cot when his brother came along, and Wood decided it was time to move on. "I sold the boat to a lovely girl who sailed off into the sunset, which I think is the best way. It felt like closing a chapter on my life."

Today, Wood lives in a cozy cottage in North London that is equally special and in some ways, quite similar to her boat—"it's heated by a wood fire too, and the downstairs is all one room." But there are aspects of her former life that can't be replicated on land: "I miss the light reflecting off the water and onto the ceiling in summer, and the ducks outside the window. And I miss the idea of being able to move on at any minute, taking my home with me." ~

MAKEOVER FOR A COZY CRUISER

At a time of rising housing costs, one of the most popular vessels providing alternative dwellings in Britain's cities is the traditional narrowboat, whose distinctive design is made to fit the country's narrow canals. In Manchester, Hester Cox, a houseboat novice, took on her first narrowboat project in 1989 and completed it over three years. Measuring around

Cox. Working with a limited budget, she spent her weekends transforming "Gloria" into a cozy abode. A hard-wearing bamboo floor now complements the glossy pine interior for rustic warmth, while vintage black and white tiles and floral curtains add an elegant, homely feel. White cabinetry accents help to make the narrow space seem more generous.

2 m (6.8 ft.) wide by 17.4 m (56.9 ft.) long, the second-hand vessel was "a nicotine stained mess—but I could see the boat was solid and well made, and there was something about the high gloss, pine, tongue and groove that I really liked," said

The houseboat was outfitted with full amenities—gas central heating and a solid-fuel stove, along with a modern shower, sink, and plumbed-in cassette toilet—perfect for both mild-weather cruising and as a stationary houseboat during the winter. ~

FROM HOME
TO BUSINESS

In Gloria, every inch of space is put to good use, with built-in cabinets and a sofa that folds out into a second berth. Gloria's owner, Hester Cox, went on to renovate further houseboats and now has her own narrowboat holiday company.

NARROWBOAT – *Manchester, United Kingdom*   228

CLEVER ICE-BREAKER

"Liz" is a repurposed canal icebreaker that dates back to 1908, measures around 11 m (36 ft.) long and 1.8 m (5.9 ft.) wide, and was completed in 2016. With its riveted iron hull, the boat was originally used to open up frozen canals for passage by other boats during the winter, and its empty shell was found during an exploration of the waterways in the former coal-mining regions of northern England. Italian-born, London-based industrial designer

Marco Monterzino transformed it into a compact, contemporary dwelling where old meets new and style meets function. "The goal was to create a living space that would provide all dry land comforts in 18 m² (194 ft.²), would work within a tight budget and time-frame, and would also embrace and enhance the historic fabric of the vessel," explains Monterzino. The predominantly white interior aims to amplify the perception of light and space within the open-plan layout that reaches uninterrupted from stern to bow. Bespoke cabinetry in dark wood »

The interior was remodeled within a strict budget and timeframe, enhancing the historical fabric of the vessel with a clean and functional interior. White walls amplify space and light, while dark wood cabinetry provides stylish storage.

» tones optimizes storage efficiency and underscores the rustic feel without becoming overbearing. High-efficiency insulation, solar panels, and onboard systems make it possible to cruise the capital's waterways and live off the grid for about two weeks at a time. ~

NARROWBOAT – *London, United Kingdom*

OFF-GRID WATERFRONT LIVING

The "River Den" (called "La Tannière" in French) is docked on the Gatineau River in the picturesque village of Wakefield, Quebec. Owner Bonnie Vanasse designed and built the houseboat over the course of four months together with her friend Denis Tremblay, who has four self-built houseboats of his own moored at the same location. "The 'River Den' was created to feel like a tree fort while having the functionality of a four-season cabin,

with a lil' Huckleberry Finn feel to it all," says Vanasse. Measuring 10 × 3.4 m (33 × 11 ft.), the houseboat floats on five high-performance pontoons and is well insulated to withstand the cold winters. Decidedly off-grid, it has no electricity, fridge, or running water. (Solar panels are an eventuality.) Large windows, rustic furnishings and fittings, and the rooftop and front decks bring comfort and character. Clever details   »

DECIDEDLY OFF-GRID, IT HAS NO ELECTRICITY, FRIDGE, OR RUNNING WATER.

»   include the steel grill floor of the loft bedroom, which allows heat from the antique wood-burning stove to circulate, and dust to fall down to the first floor for easy cleaning. A pump draws river water into the kitchen sink for dishwashing. The wedge roof can be removed to make the structure road-legal for easy land transport. ~

FLOATING CABIN – *Gatineau River, Quebec, Canada*   236

THE RIVER DEN WAS CREATED TO FEEL LIKE A TREE FORT WHILE HAVING THE FUNCTIONALITY OF A FOUR-SEASON CABIN

Above: A pump draws river water into the kitchen sink for dish washing. **Right:** The steel grill floor of the loft bedroom allows heat from the antique wood-burning stove to circulate.

FLOATING CABIN – *Gatineau River, Quebec, Canada*

PARISIAN CHIC

Interior designer Valérie Mazerat captured the spirit of Parisian chic in the cozy Dutch barge she renovated to live in with her young daughter. She didn't start entirely from scratch for its unique look: the previous owner of the boat, which dates back to the early 1900s, extended the upper level living space by integrating a 1920s train carriage on the top deck. Mazerat spent two years giving the boat a thorough makeover. Mazerat's charcoal gray interior and steel elements

pay tribute to the vessel's industrial past without feeling cold. Warm neutrals, bright accents, and soft and hard furniture with vintage design pieces establish a vibe that is both cozy and sophisticated. At the back of the boat is the living room with two day beds, space-saving bookshelves over the windows, and a wood-burning stove. A custom-made dining table and galley lead up to the wheelhouse. Bedrooms are on the lower level, with portholes bringing in natural light. The front of the boat serves as the perfect sun deck with a canopy-covered space for sleeping on hot summer nights. Moored in a   »»

The charcoal gray interior and steel elements pay tribute to the vessel's industrial past, while warm neutrals, bright accents, and vintage design pieces establish a cozy yet sophisticated vibe.

»»   canal off the Seine at Bassin de l'Arsenal, the houseboat shares views of the Place de la Bastille with around 200 other vessels. "It's one of the city's best kept secrets," Mazerat says of the marina. "It's another world … There's a sense of freedom you don't get living ashore." ~

FLOATING AGAINST THE GRAIN

Retrouvius, an architectural salvage and design studio selling reconditioned furniture and fittings in London, designed the interior of this floating guest house in the Cotswolds in south-

central England. Reclaimed timber and tiles were used in combination with a harmonious blend of warm, natural textures and tones for a contemporary, rustic indoor experience. "The colors are so much richer in old materials," says Maria Speake, who founded the studio with Adam Hills in 1997. In the kitchen, reclaimed Spanish wood-look ceramic tiles complement a patchwork of wooden floorboards repurposed as wall cladding and cabinets. On the outside, the two-room, 50 m² (538 ft.²) modern dwelling clad in pale wood has an insulating green roof and a panel of large windows and doors that reveal views of pastoral beauty. The project was realized in collaboration with Eco Pavilions, a "collaborative team »»

"THE COLORS ARE SO MUCH RICHER IN OLD MATERIALS."

FLOATING CABIN – *Cotswolds, United Kingdom*

RECLAIMED TIMBER AND TILES WERE USED IN COMBINATION WITH A HARMONIOUS BLEND OF WARM, NATURAL TEXTURE.

» of designers, architects, engineers, artists, builders, and makers" specializing in bespoke floating homes, offices, retreats, and pavilions. The structures are hand built in the company's workshop in Hertfordshire north of London, using responsibly sourced materials according to ethical work practices. ~

DIY FLOATING STUDIO

"Anyone can build a boat," claims photographer Claudius Schulze. Fed up with a lack of affordable space for artistic creation in Hamburg, Schulze built his own floating studio, named "Eroberung des Unwahrscheinlichen"

or "Conquest of the Improbable". With no prior boat-building experience, the project seemed far-fetched when he began with the construction in March 2016. But with the clever use of recycled material and the help of skilled friends, half a year and 7.500€ later his vessel was shipshape. Equipped with solar panels, a water recycling system and a compost toilet the boat is nearly self-sufficient. In 2017, Claudius Schulze fitted the boat with an off-the-shelf outboard engine and embarked on a Tour-de-Europe that brought him through Amsterdam and Paris. As Schulze's photographic work focusses on the state of nature and the societal changes caused by climate change and digitalization, he sees the boat as a practical exploration of the topic, a space where he can »»»

»   develop and tests new concepts and ideas that will eventually re-surface in his artistic work.

Schulze would like to see more affordable, undetermined spaces in Hamburg's harbor to offer room for the city's creative potential to unfold. According to Schulze, "What's the point if an artist has a place to live but can't afford a studio? Hamburg shouldn't only be a residential city. ∼

THROUGH EUROPE'S CANALS

Claudius's one-eared cat feels at home on board. As part of the "Übermut" project, they travelled together from Hamburg to Amsterdam's "Unseen Photo Fair" and on to "Paris Photo". Visitors are always welcome on board for a dialogue on vision, formation, creation and environment.

INDEX

ROCK THE BOAT

Boats, Cabins and Homes on the Water

This book was conceived, edited, and designed by **Gestalten.**

Edited by **Robert Klanten** and **Maximilian Funk**

Written by **Alisa Kotmair**

Project Management by **Adam Jackman**

Creative Direction of Design by **Ludwig Wendt**
Layout and Cover by **Léon Giogoli**

Typefaces:
Adorn Smooth Condensed by **Laura Worthington Type**;
Metallophile by **Mark Simonson Studio**

Cover photography by **Kevin McElvaney**

Printed by **Offsetdruckerei Grammlich**, Pliezhausen
Made in Germany

Published by **Gestalten**, Berlin 2017
ISBN 978-3-89955-916-3

2nd printing, 2018

Respect copyrights, encourage creativity!
For more information, and to order books, please visit www.gestalten.com.

Bibliographic information published by the Deutsche Nationalbibliothek.
The Deutsche Nationalbibliothek lists this publication in the Deutsche Nationalbibliografie; detailed bibliographic data are available online at http://dnb.d-nb.de.

None of the content in this book was published in exchange for payment by commercial parties or designers; Gestalten selected all included work based solely on its artistic merit.

This book was printed on paper certified according to the standards of the FSC®.

FSC
www.fsc.org
MIX
Paper from responsible sources
FSC® C011712